D1710528

To: ____________________

From: ____________________

Together is Better

Together is Better

A Little Book of Inspiration

SIMON SINEK

Illustrated by Ethan M. Aldridge

Portfolio / Penguin

An imprint of Penguin Random House LLC
penguinrandomhouse.com

Illustrations by Ethan M. Aldridge
Lines from *Together Is Better*, written by Dela Fumador
and arranged by Aloe Blacc © Aloe Blacc Publishing, Inc.

Library of Congress Cataloging-in-Publication Data

Names: Sinek, Simon, author.
Title: Together is better : a little book of inspiration / Simon Sinek ; illustrated by Ethan M. Aldridge.
Description: New York : Portfolio/Penguin, [2016]
Identifiers: LCCN 2016031125| ISBN 9780698194298 (ebook) | ISBN 9781591847854 (hardcover)
Subjects: LCSH: Organizational behavior. | Organizational change. | Job satisfaction. | Leadership.
Classification: LCC HD58.7 .S5933 2016 | DDC 650.1—dc23
LC record available at https://lccn.loc.gov/2016031125

Printed in the United States of America
9 10 8

Creative direction by Christopher Sergio
Book design by Daniel Lagin

For Sara

I'll follow you anywhere

Contents

Together is Better

Hello

It feels nice to feel inspired. It feels amazing to feel inspired by our work.

This idea is core to the vision I imagine: to build a world in which the vast majority of us wake up every single morning inspired to go to work, feel safe when we're there and return home fulfilled at the end of the day.

Building this world will not be easy, nor will it happen in a year or two. But if we commit to working together, to each do our part to help advance a shared vision, we can build this world we imagine.

It is this journey that I hope to capture in this book.

This is the story of three friends who live in a place that is fine. Not great—just fine. Though they find moments of happiness on the playground, they, like all the kids, live in the shadow of the "king of the playground." He cares mostly about himself and his own status and leads through fear. As a result, the other kids stick to themselves for fear of being singled out for attention.

This story is a metaphor.

The playground represents the organizations we work for, especially the ones with unhealthy work environments. The king of the playground represents our boss, or our company—who seem to care more about numbers than people, who lead by intimidation or simply have no idea how to create a place where we are inspired to come every single day. (Or maybe they just don't care.) The playground politics are the office politics that many of us experience in our jobs on a daily basis. We go to a place where gossip, blame shifting and self-interest have overrun shared vision, trust and cooperation.

And, like the kids on the playground, most of us put up with it. It's fine, we say when someone asks us if we like our jobs, same as every day. Not great—just fine.

Some of us dream of quitting or finding something better. Some of us put up with what we have, rationalizing that we have bills to pay or mouths to feed. The question is: can we change our lot?

The three friends, our three heroes, are archetypes who represent us. At various points in our careers we have been each one of them. They dream of leaving the playground like we dream of a different or better place to work. And even if they make it out of the playground, even if we leave our job in search of something better, the question is: where are we going and how will we get there?

This page is infused with a scent—the smell of optimism, to be exact. It was designed to set the tone, to evoke a feeling, that will prepare you for the journey on which you are about to embark.

To activate it, all you need to do is gently run your finger across the page, then lift the book up to your nose, close your eyes and smell.

If you aren't interested in smelling anything before you read the book, then simply turn the page and continue as you normally would.

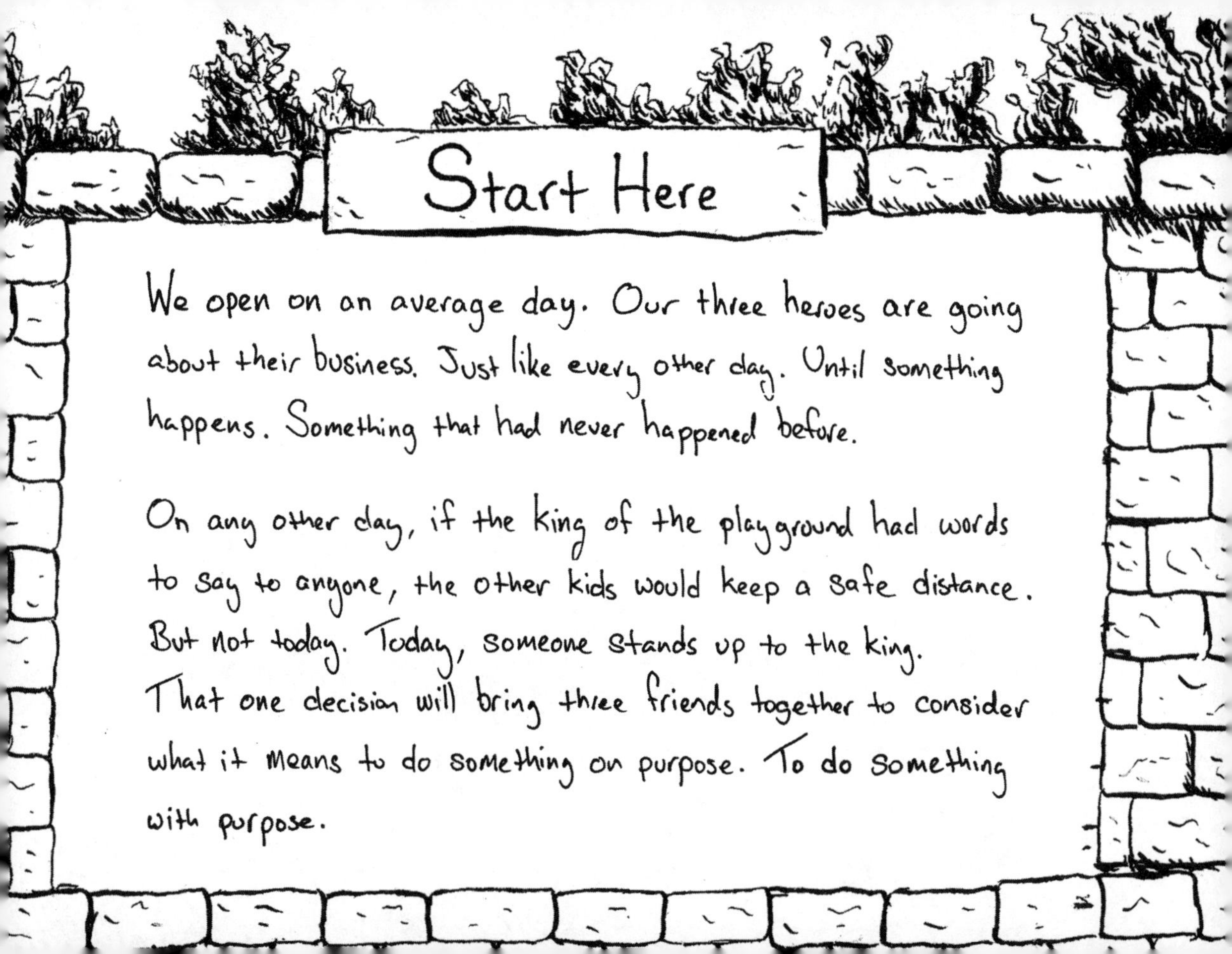
Start Here
We open on an average day. Our three heroes are going about their business. Just like every other day. Until something happens. Something that had never happened before.
On any other day, if the king of the playground had words to say to anyone, the other kids would keep a safe distance. But not today. Today, someone stands up to the king. That one decision will bring three friends together to consider what it means to do something on purpose. To do something with purpose.

Most of us live our lives by accident—we live as it happens. Fulfillment comes when we live our lives on purpose.

If you say your job is something you "don't plan on doing forever," then why are you doing it now?

Leadership is not
about being in charge.
Leadership is about
taking care of those
in your charge.

"There's only one way to avoid criticism:
do nothing, say nothing, and be nothing."

—Aristotle

Leadership is not a rank or position to be attained. Leadership is a service to be given.

Under poor leaders we feel like we work for the company.
With good leaders we feel like we work for each other.

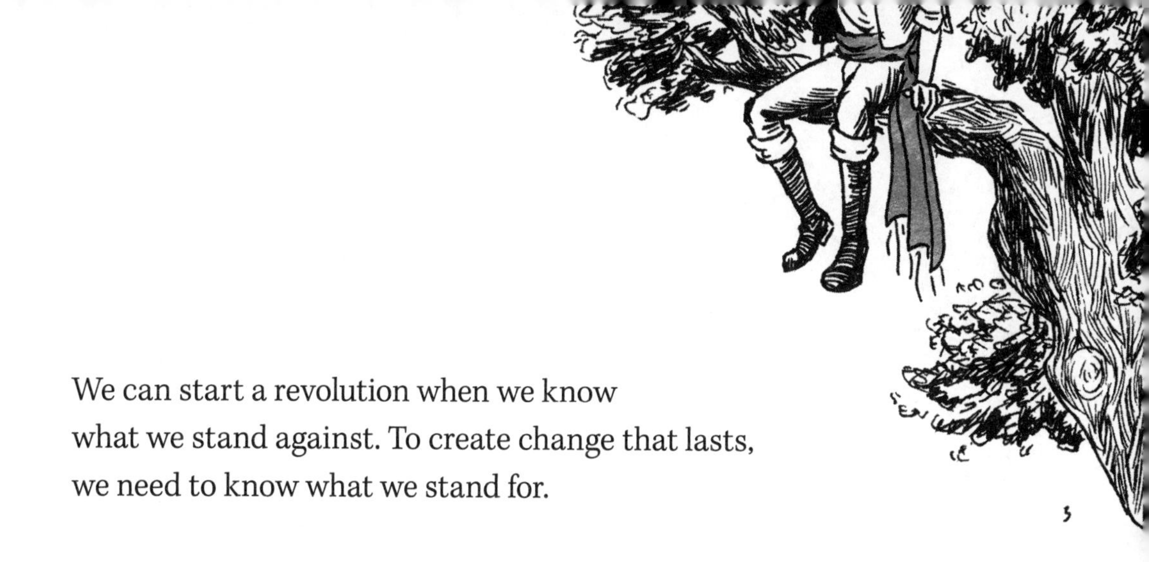

We can start a revolution when we know
what we stand against. To create change that lasts,
we need to know what we stand for.

A vision is like a dream—it will disappear unless we do something with it. Do something big or do something small. But stop wondering and go on an adventure.

That idea is so fantastic.
Stop talking about it and do it.

Genius is in the idea.
Impact comes from action.

Pick One: Go Alone or Go Together

It's all fine and good to imagine what life would be like somewhere else. It takes some courage to leave and go somewhere new. To head out to the great unknown. But what happens if upon taking the first step, something goes wrong? Maybe it was a bad idea to leave in the first place? Maybe it's best to turn back and stay put? After all, the devil you know is better than the devil you don't.

Or maybe, if you have the right people with you, they will give you the courage to keep going.

It doesn't matter when we start.
It doesn't matter where we start.
All that matters is that we start.

What good is having a belly if there's no fire in it?
Wake up, drink your passion, light a match and get to work!

We achieve more when we chase the dream instead of the competition.

Safe is good for sidewalks and swimming pools.
Life requires risk if we are to get anywhere.

Leaders give us the chance to try and fail,
then give us another chance to try and succeed.

Find a Vision

There are two ways to go on a journey – walk away from something or go towards something. But what if you don't know where to go? "Find a job you love," we're told. "Find your passion and do that," they say. All good advice and perfectly useless.

If we knew that, we wouldn't feel the way we do now. Plus, we can spend a lifetime trying to answer that question...

... or we can find someone who already has an answer, as our three friends will soon discover.

Discontent can easily drive us to walk away. But only with a clear vision, no matter from where or from whom it comes, can we find the inspiration to set ourselves on a journey to go towards something greater.

When we say out loud what we don't know, it increases the likelihood that someone who does know will offer help.

Innovators are the ones whose dreams are clearer than the reality that tells them they're crazy.

The best way to find out if it will work is to do it.

Always plan for the fact that no plan ever goes according to plan.

If the challenge we face doesn't scare us, then it's probably not that important.

When we are closed to ideas, what we hear is criticism.
When we are open to criticism, what we get is advice.

Bad leaders care about who's right.
Good leaders care about what's right.

Don't complain, contribute.

Persevere

Life is difficult and dangerous. Anyone who would attempt to do it alone is simply mad. We know to always do difficult things with a buddy. So if the journey of life is to be filled with setbacks and disappointments, with confusion and uncertainty, it makes sense that we should trust others to join us on the journey.

As individuals, we're useless. We can't lift heavy weight and we can't solve complex problems. But together?

Together we are remarkable.

Bad teams work in the same place.
Good teams work together.

The ability of a group of people to do remarkable things hinges on how well those people can pull together as a team.

You can't do it alone. So don't pretend you can.

Together is better.

A team is not a group of people who work together.
A team is a group of people who trust each other.

A good leader doesn't only inspire us to have confidence in what they can do.
A great leader inspires us to have confidence in what we can do.

Success is when reality looks like what's in our imagination.

Excitement comes from the achievement. Fulfillment comes from the journey that got you there.

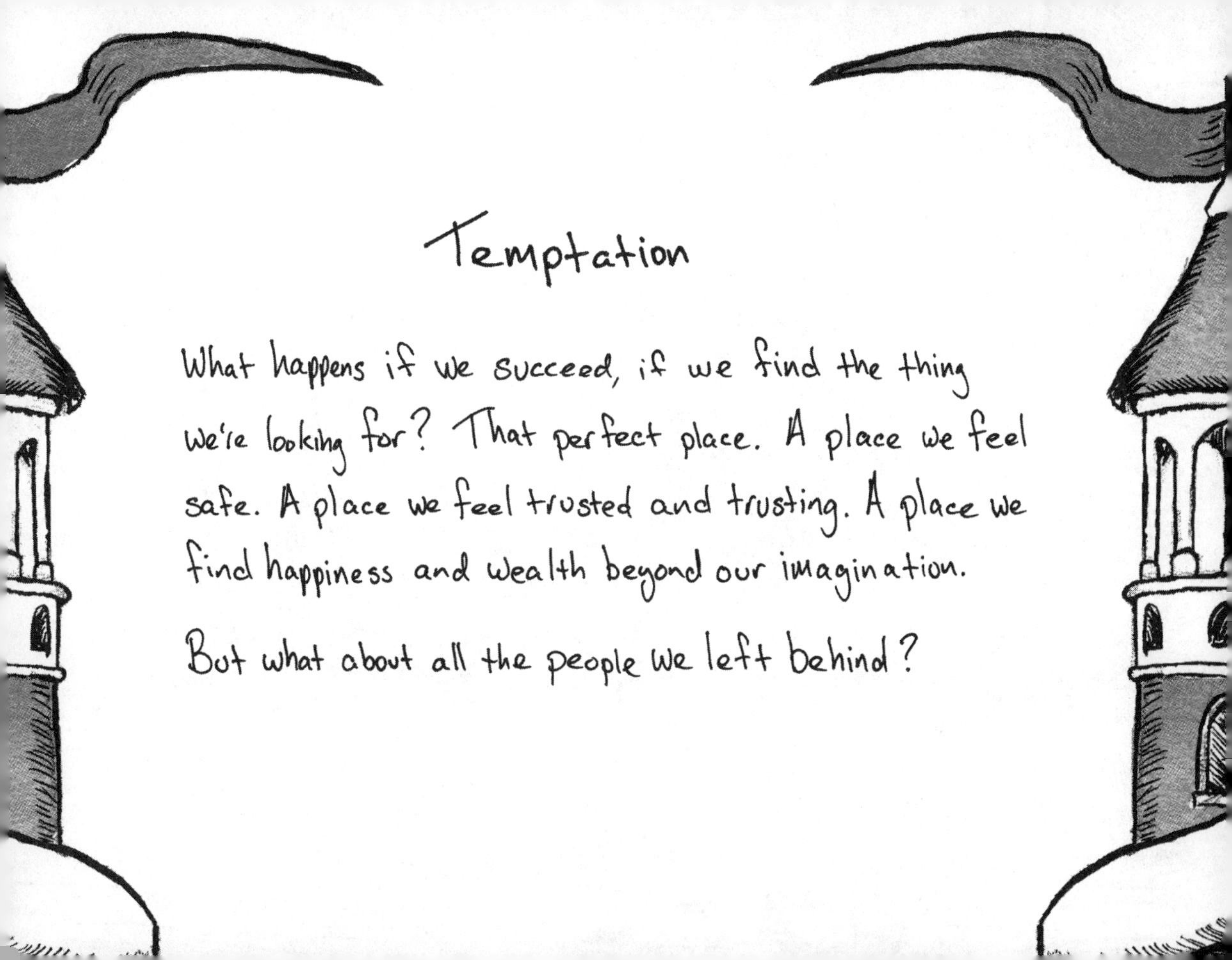
Temptation
What happens if we succeed, if we find the thing we're looking for? That perfect place. A place we feel safe. A place we feel trusted and trusting. A place we find happiness and wealth beyond our imagination.
But what about all the people we left behind?

Our greatest test may not come from the path we travel to success. Our greatest test is what we do with success once we find it.

The value of our lives is not determined by what we do for ourselves.
The value of our lives is determined by what we do for others.

The opportunity is not to discover the perfect company for ourselves.
The opportunity is to build the perfect company for each other.

The Return

Leadership is a daily practice. The more we practice working to consider the lives of others, even if it comes at the expense of our interests, the better we get at it. Like a muscle, the more we practice leadership the stronger we get. More important, the stronger we get, the stronger those around us become too. It is at this point that the overwhelming challenges we faced as individuals, as if by magic, become simple to solve for the team.

It is a luxury to put our interests first. It is an honor to put the interests of others before ourselves.

Our struggles are the short-term steps we must take on our way to long-term success.

Leadership is an education. And the best leaders think of themselves as the students, not the teachers.

Fulfillment is not born of the dream.
Fulfillment is born of the journey.

Life is beautiful not because of the things we see or the things we do.
Life is beautiful because of the people we meet.

True strength is the courage to admit weakness.

Failure we can do alone.

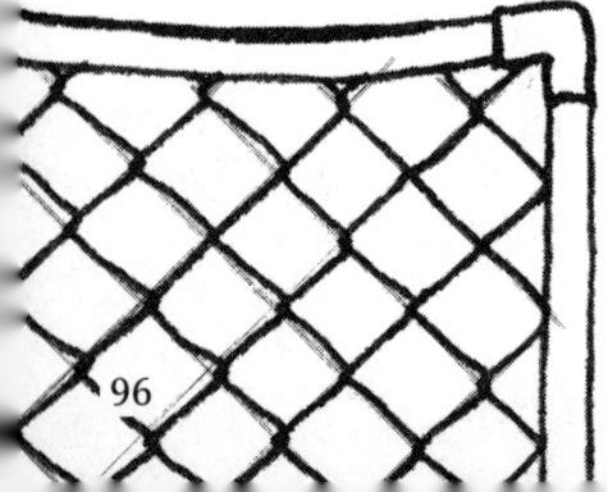

Success always takes help.

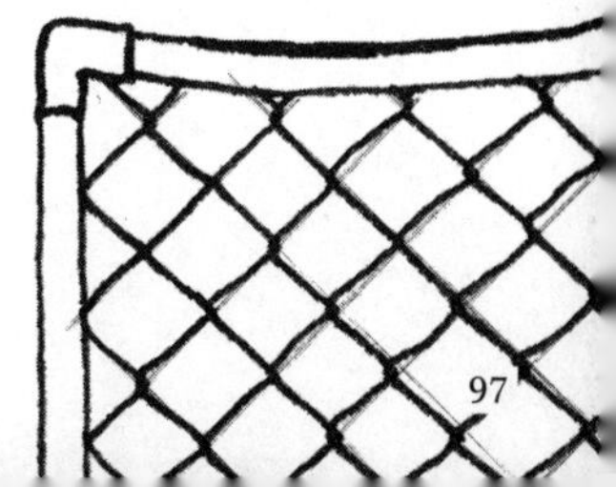

A boss has the title. A leader has the people.

The true value of a leader is not measured by the work they do. The true value of a leader is measured by the work they inspire others to do.

When we tell people to do their jobs, we get workers.
When we trust people to get the job done, we get leaders.

Working hard for something we don't care about is called stress.
Working hard for something we love is called passion.

Be the Leader You Wish You Had
The greatest joy a leader has is to become the one who helps others find the vision they are looking for.
To see those in their charge do more than they thought they were capable of.
To watch the group take care of each other. To see the team work together to solve unsolvable problems.
This is what it means to become a leader. It is not a journey to rise in the ranks, it is the journey to help those around us rise.

The mind can be convinced but the heart must be won.

A star wants to see himself rise to the top. A leader wants to see those around him become stars.

A leader must be inspired by the people before a leader can inspire the people.

"To go fast, go alone. To go far, go together."

—African proverb

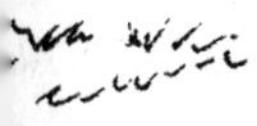

A Little More

It was such a joy to write this book—to share a little inspiration in such a simple format. That said, when we were done writing it, we realized that some of the quotes and illustrations had some nuance to them that was lost in this format. So, we decided to share a little more about some of the ideas. Hope you enjoy.

Page 6 | **Most of us live our lives by accident—we live as it happens. Fulfillment comes when we live our lives on purpose.**

Page 8 | **If you say your job is something you "don't plan on doing forever," then why are you doing it now?**

The ideas in the opening quotes of the book capture the foundation of my beliefs—that fulfillment is a right and not a privilege. I think too many of us confuse the excitement of a job—winning a new client, getting a promotion or a bonus, hitting the goal—with the deep sense of joy that can come from the work we do. That feeling of love for and from our colleagues, that feeling of contribution to something bigger than ourselves, that feeling that we are valued and valuable.

We do not have to accept the hand we are dealt—we have options and we have choices, and most of all, we have a perspective. We have a say in how the time we spend at work should feel. It is a sense of purpose, cause, or belief—a certainty of *Why* we do what we do—that underlies fulfillment. And we can demand it.

Page 9 | **Leadership is not about being in charge. Leadership is about taking care of those in your charge.**

There is no nuance here. This idea is pretty clear. I guess I'm just amazed that in this modern day and age in which there are so many good books, TED talks, Twitter feeds and *Harvard Business Review* articles about what leadership really is, some people still think they are leaders simply because they got a promotion. (OK, little rant over.)

Page 15 | **We can start a revolution when we know what we stand against. To create change that lasts, however, we need to know what we stand for.**

The importance of knowing where we are going, not simply what we are running from or trying to change, is one of those nuances that a poetic little quote can't fully capture. This is one of the reasons I love the Declaration of Independence. It was a document that articulated the thing we wanted to do . . . even before we did it. All of the grievances listed in it about how King George led came after the ideal state of "All men are created equal." In writing it, the founding fathers prioritized what we stood for over what we were against.

Social media is great for rallying people. It can incite people to act

and break something or change something, even for the better. But it doesn't and can't inspire the hard work that needs to be done to build something.

The reason we more often rally against something is because it's easier. It's easier to stoke someone's fears, discomfort or sense of injustice because the thing that they fear, that makes them uncomfortable or that they feel is unfair is usually a real thing.

Standing for something is often more abstract. Something that may be clear in the minds of the visionaries may seem distant, elusive or just plain impossible to the rest of us. It is the responsibility of the visionary to paint the abstract future as if it were the tangible present. Then we will have something to rally for.

Page 16 | **A vision is like a dream—it will disappear unless we do something with it. Do something big or do something small. But stop wondering and go on an adventure.**

I love this picture. This is the one I had printed and have hanging on the wall. It reminds me that when obstacles appear in life, the fun is figuring out ways over and around instead of focusing on what's in the way. We can imagine what's over the wall or we can stand there and stare at the wall. The choice is ours.

Page 19 | **That idea is so fantastic. Stop talking about it and do it.**

Yup.

Page 29 | **We achieve more when we chase the dream instead of the competition.**

There is a difference between companies that have internal politics and companies that have purpose and cause. The people inside the companies with politics are fighting against themselves. The ones with purpose are fighting together.

It's the same with companies obsessed with their competitors versus companies obsessed with their vision. (Aside: "being number 1" is not a vision.) Companies obsessed with what their competition is doing are always reacting or trying to outpace another company. Companies obsessed with their vision are always working to outpace themselves.

These companies also understand that sometimes they are ahead and sometimes they are behind. Less distracted with the ups and downs of the short-term, their obsession is the long-term. It's the difference between trying to win every battle and trying to win the war . . . and no one knows when the war will end. This is why the visionary companies eventually outpace and outlast their competition.

Page 35 | **Find a Vision**

We were very particular when we named this section "find" a vision instead of "have" a vision. For some reason, there is this standard in business that has emerged that we all have to "have" a vision. Some big, bold, change-the-world Steve-Jobsian vision. Not only is that totally unrealistic, it's a lot of stress for the vast majority of us who aren't Steve Jobs.

I am more comfortable declaring that we should all *find* a vision.

There are definitely visionaries out there—people who have a sense of a different future and the ability to express it. If we like their vision, then we can choose to follow them or their vision. Their vision becomes ours and we can use it to navigate our choices.

It is just as inspiring to follow a vision that resonates with us as it is to have our own. Martin Luther King Jr., Gandhi, Thomas Jefferson, Richard Branson, Warren Buffett and Elon Musk all expressed their visions and did things that inspired others to follow them. Some of their followers bought their products. Some of their followers joined their organizations. Some of their followers were simply inspired by one of these leaders and did things to help contribute to the vision. Regardless—all these followers *found* a vision and chose to follow it. They didn't have to come up with one themselves.

And here's the best part—it's the followers, not the visionary, who bring the vision to life. Visionaries need followers as much as followers need a vision.

So . . . who inspires you?

Page 37 | **When we say out loud what we don't know, it increases the likelihood that someone who does know will offer help.**

The single most powerful lesson I ever learned in my life is that I don't have to know all the answers. And when I don't, I don't have to pretend that I do.

There was a time in my career that I thought I had to know all the answers because I was running the account or running the business.

The problem was, it was a total lie. No one knows all the answers and no one has perfect clarity. I had to learn that lesson the hard way.

As soon as I mustered the courage to state out loud what I didn't know or understand, or ask for help or accept it when it was offered, my career completely turned around. It turns out, there were always people who wanted to help . . . they just didn't know I needed it. Funny that.

Page 38 | **Innovators are the ones whose dreams are clearer than the reality that tells them they're crazy.**

If anyone has any ideas on how to put punctuation in this thought to make it a little easier to understand the first time you read it, please let me know.

Page 46 | **When we are closed to ideas, what we hear is criticism. When we are open to criticism, what we get is advice.**

Very often we will offer well-intentioned advice to someone and they take it as criticism. Our temptation is to defend our advice, or worse, we find ourselves sucked into an argument.

If someone takes our advice as a criticism, it may be because of our delivery. Or maybe we touched a nerve . . . or maybe there is something about which they are unsure or insecure . . . or maybe it's the twelfth time they've tried to fix it, which is why they got defensive in the first place. If that happens, it's a great opportunity to practice a little empathy, to try to understand the thing they are reacting to. Then, and only then, will our words become advice.

Page 72 | **Excitement comes from the achievement. Fulfillment comes from the journey that got you there.**

Winning the award is exciting. But the real fulfillment comes from looking back and seeing all the people who rooted for you, helped you, put their reputations on the line for you. All the people who believed in you.

It's ironic; the things we think will be defining moments when we look ahead in our lives rarely are. More often than not, when we look back at our achievements, the defining moments were the experiences that led up to those big achievements. The lessons learned.

It's worth stating again—finding excitement at work comes from the win, hitting the goal, getting the promotion. It's the hit of dopamine. But fulfillment—that true, oxytocin-driven, life-lasting joy—comes from the quality of the relationships we make as we struggle over every obstacle along the way *and* the feelings we share when we win together.

Page 79 | **The value of our lives is not determined by what we do for ourselves. The value of our lives is determined by what we do for others.**

How should we ask people to judge our legacies? By the balance in our bank accounts on the day we die? The number of emails we answered? How many times we went to the gym? Or by the character of the children we raised and the people we led, or the impact we had in the lives of the people around us?

Let us live our lives for the legacies we want to leave.

Page 80 | **The opportunity is not to discover the perfect company for ourselves. The opportunity is to build the perfect company for each other.**

There is a whole section in the bookshop called "self-help," but there is no section called "help others." The irony is that success and joy actually come from the service we offer to others. It's not "how can I lose ten pounds?" it's "how can I help my friend feel healthy and strong?" It's not "how can I find my dream job?" it's "how can I help someone I care about find their calling?"

It's the act of service, not the selfish pursuit, that actually helps us solve the same problems we may face in our own lives more effectively. What's more, it turns a short-term, selfish goal into something bigger, longer lasting, and more noble.

If we go to work and don't love our jobs, quitting is not the only option. We can choose to commit ourselves to ensuring that our colleagues love coming to work. Our work becomes helping them to find *their* calling. That act of service not only changes the way our coworkers feel about their jobs; it actually changes the way we feel about ours.

That act of service is called leadership.

Page 86 | **Our struggles are the short-term steps we must take on our way to long-term success.**

There's an old story about a Chinese farmer whose horse escaped into the hills. When his neighbors expressed their sympathy for his bad luck, he told them, "Bad luck? Good luck? Who knows?" Soon the horse returned with a herd of wild horses from the hills. When his neighbors congratulated the farmer on his good luck, he told them, "Good luck? Bad luck? Who knows?"

The farmer's son worked to break the horses, and instead fell and broke his leg. When the neighbors expressed their sympathy for his bad luck, he told them, "Bad luck? Good luck? Who knows?" While the son was healing, the army arrived and officers conscripted every able-bodied young man in the village. Since his son was not taken, his neighbors congratulated the farmer on his good luck. He told them, "Good luck? Bad luck? Who knows?"

Life is not a single scene. It is a whole movie that must play out . . . our only challenge (or opportunity) is we don't know what comes next.

Page 89 | **Leadership is an education. And the best leaders think of themselves as the students, not the teachers.**

If you have a new idea or perspective to offer and you repeatedly hear, "I've been doing this a lot longer than you—I think I know what I'm doing," RUN! RUN AWAY!

Page 95 | **True strength is the courage to admit weakness.**

Being vulnerable doesn't mean we have to cry more or act meek. Being vulnerable means admitting we don't know something or that we made a mistake. It's asking for help. These simple expressions make us vulnerable because they leave us open to criticism, humiliation or attack. If, however, we work in a strong culture, among others around whom we feel safe, expressing vulnerability is the most powerful feeling in the world. We feel the love and support from those around us. We open ourselves to learning and growth. And our simple admission invites others to help us . . . thus enhancing our chances for success.

And here's the best part. Our courage to be the first one to express vulnerability inspires those around us to take the same risks. And when they do, the team will rally to support them as well . . . and the whole organization thrives.

And that's the irony. Lying, hiding and faking might make us *appear* stronger, but it ultimately undermines the culture. The courage to be vulnerable *actually* makes the organization, and all the teams within it, stronger and higher performing.

Page 103 | **When we tell people to do their jobs, we get workers. When we trust people to get the job done, we get leaders.**

To become a leader, we have to go through a transition. Some go through it quickly. Some go through it slowly. And, unfortunately, some never go through it at all.

When we are junior, our only job is to be good at our job. When we're junior, our companies will give us lots of training—how to use the software, how to sell, how to make a presentation—so that we will be good at our job. Some even get advanced degrees so they can be even better at their job—accountants or engineers, for example. And if we are good at our job, the company will promote us. And if we are *really* good at our job, eventually we get promoted to a position where we become responsible for the people who do the job we used to do. But very few companies teach us how to do *that.* Very few companies teach us how to lead. That's like putting someone at a machine and demanding results without showing them how the machine works.

That's why we get managers and not leaders inside companies. Because the person who got promoted really does know how to do our job better than we do . . . that's what got them promoted in the first place. Of course they are going to tell us how we "should" do things. They manage us because no one taught them how to lead us.

This is one of the hardest lessons to learn when we get promoted to a position of leadership—that we are no longer responsible for doing the job, we are now responsible for the people who do the job. There isn't a CEO on the planet who is responsible for the customer. CEOs are responsible for the people who are responsible for the customer. Get that right, and everybody wins—employees and customers.

Leadership is hard work. Not the hard work of doing the job—it's the hard work of learning to let go. It's the hard work of training people, coaching people, believing in people and trusting people. Leadership is a human activity. And, unlike the job, leadership lasts beyond whatever happens during the workday.

Page 108 | **The mind can be convinced but the heart must be won.**

My editor, Eric, loves this quote. He thinks it is the underlying thought of all my books and all my work.

I guess I won him over.

Page 113 | **A leader must be inspired by the people before a leader can inspire the people.**

Leadership is like being a parent. Everyone has the capacity to be a parent, but not everyone wants to be a parent or should be a parent. Likewise, everyone has the capacity to be a leader, but not everyone wants to be a leader or should be a leader.

The joy of parenting doesn't come from the work of being a parent, it comes from seeing our children do things that delight us. Like when we catch our five-year-old sharing with our four-year-old. Like when we attend school plays or graduations or when they say funny things or find their first boyfriends and girlfriends.

Leadership is exactly the same. The joy of leadership comes from seeing someone on our team achieve more than they thought they were capable of. When we see our team come together to solve the impossible problem. When the team forms deep bonds of trust and would do anything to help each other out.

The more we are inspired by the amazingness of our people, the more we can inspire them.

"TOGETHER IS BETTER"

written by Dela Fumador
arranged by Aloe Blacc

To hear the song that goes with this book,
visit AloeBlacc.com/togetherisbetter

The scented page in this book has been infused with the smell of optimism. It was specially designed by the geniuses at 12.29.

Learn more about what they do at 1229.com.

What good is an idea if it remains an idea?
Try. Experiment. Iterate. Fail. Try again.
Change the world.

If this book inspired you, please pass it on to someone you want to inspire.